MODERN PUBLISHING'S UNOFFICIAL
Yu-Gi-O!
GUIDEBOOK

This is an unofficial and unauthorized project. No persons associated with Yu-Gi-Oh have given their permission to publish this book or are in any way connected with it. Although the publishers believe the contents of this book to be true at the time of publication, they do not accept any responsibility in this regard.

Modern Publishing
A Division of Unisystems, Inc.
New York, New York 10022
Printed in the U.S.A.
Series UPC: 65025

Going First or Second in a Duel:
What's best?

By Professor Duel

So, you have your deck put together and you're at your local tournament. You've just won the coin toss and now you have to decide if you want to go first or second. The answer seems easy: "Of course I want to go first!" But do you really want to? Going first or second each have their advantages and disadvantages that are mostly based on the type of deck you use and your style of duelling. So before you go rushing into this decision, read this first.

Before you start your duel, official tournament rules state that you and your opponent must determine who is going first by flipping a coin. The winner of the coin toss gets to pick. In my experience, most duelists prefer to go first rather than second, so let's discuss the tactical reasons for this.

First Turn Strategies

Although you can't attack if you go first and you might end up revealing some of your strategy, when you go first you are free to set up your field without having to worry about one of your magic cards being countered or any of your monsters being destroyed by a pesky Trap Hole. Great cards to have for a first turn start would be Man-Eater Bug, Pot of Greed, Graceful Charity, Imperial Order, Trap Hole, Penguin Soldier, Hane-Hane, Mirror Force. Basically any card that will let you destroy your opponent's monster or counter their onslaught when they go next is great . . . that's actually true for any turn. The key about going first and getting these cards is that if you can keep your opponent off balance from the start of the duel, then victory will most likely be yours. Here are some examples:

• Set a Man-Eater Bug, Hane-Hane, Penguin Soldier (or any card that will get their monster off the field) face down on your first turn.

Clear the Monster zone with the effect of that card on your next turn, and then attack your opponent's Life Points directly.

• Another way to execute this same strategy is to set up a trap for them. Put down something like Trap Hole or Mirror Force, then throw down a weak monster in face up attack mode and dare him to attack.

When using either of these strategies to start it helps to have a counter card down and ready, such as Imperial Order or Magic Jammer, just in case your opponent has a Raigeki or Dark Hole waiting in his hand. Also when going first, the more cards you can get in your hand to begin with, the more options you'll have for the rest of the duel. So, cards like Pot of Greed and Graceful Charity can greatly improve the chance for you to crush your opponent and keep them off balance.

Want to really surprise your opponent? If you are lucky enough to draw Card Destruction on your first turn, play it after setting and activating all the other cards in your own hand. Your opponent, who has just spent all that time looking at his five cards and planning his own opening move, will have to discard his entire hand and start over.

Just remember, when starting out first, the key to being successful is to set things up so that your opponent will be off balance and disoriented for the rest of the duel.

Second Turn Strategies

If you choose to go second, here's what you should be focusing on. Choosing to go second already messes with your opponent because most people just expect you to want to go first. Like I just said, anytime you can throw your opponent off balance by doing something unexpected is good.

A duelist who goes second has the advantage of seeing what his opponent does on his first turn, hopefully getting some insight into his strategy so he can set up your counter strikes. Going second also gives you the advantage of being able to start off your half of the duel with an attack. Cards like Dark Hole, Raigeki, Heavy Storm, Exiled Force, Tribute to the Doomed, and any high ATK four-star monsters (Gemini Elf, Spear Dragon, 7-Colored Fish) are good to have off the draw.

• If your deck has a lot of ways to remove cards from the field, then going

second should be your choice. Start by Heavy Storming the field, in case your opponent has any hidden traps waiting for you. Then destroy his monsters with Dark Hole, Tribute to the Doomed, or Raigeki and summon your own high ATK four-star monster for quick life point damage to your opponent.

• If your deck is weak with card-removal tactics, then choose to go first and set up your field with strong counter attacks, like I explained above.

One of the major disadvantages to going second is that your opponent already has their field set up and ready for an attack. So if he has a great draw right from the start, you might be in for a rough duel.

Final Thoughts

In the end choosing if you go first or second really comes down to your deck construction, how you duel, and what you prefer. But be aware that there is always an advantage—and a disadvantage—regardless of how you start your duel. So even if things don't start out the way you would have liked them to, the duel can change with the draw of one card.

2003 JOEY STARTER DECK 1ST EDITION COMPLETE SET $37.00

C= Common • UR= Ultra Rare • SC= Secret Rare • R= Rare

SDJ-001
Red Eyes B. Dragon
UR $ 7.50

SDJ-002
Swordsman of
Landstar
C $ .30

SDJ-003
Baby Dragon
C $ .30

SDJ-004
Spirit of the Harp
C $ .40

SDJ-005
Island Turtle
C $ .30

SDJ-006
Flame Manipulator
C $ .30

SDJ-007
Masaki the Legendary
Swordsman
C $ .30

SDJ-008
7 Colored Fish
C $ .50

SDJ-009
Armored Lizard
C $ .30

SDJ-010
Darkfire Soldier #1
C $ .30

SDJ-011
Harpie's Brother
C $ .30

SDJ-012
Gearfried the Iron
Knight
C $ .30

SDJ-013
Karate Man
C $ .30

SDJ-014
Milus Radiant
C $ .30

SDJ-015
Time Wizard
C $ 3.50

SDJ-016
Maha Vailo
C $ .40

SDJ-017
Magician of Faith
C $ .30

SDJ-018
Big Eye
C $ .30

SDJ-019
Sangan
C $ .50

SDJ-020
Princess of Tsurugi
C $ .30

WHITE MAGICAL HAT

[SPELLCASTER / EFFECT]
When this card inflicts damage to your opponent's Life Points, 1 card must be discarded randomly from your opponent's hand to the Graveyard.

ATK/1000 DEF/ 700

PENGUIN SOLDIER

[AQUA / EFFECT]
FLIP: You can return up to 2 Monster Cards from the field to the owner's hand.

ATK/ 750 DEF/ 500

THOUSAND DRAGON

[DRAGON / FUSION]
"Thousand Dragon" + "Baby Dragon"

ATK/2400 DEF/2000

FLAME SWORDSMAN

[WARRIOR / FUSION]
"Flame Manipulator" + "Masaki the Legendary Swordsman"

ATK/1800 DEF/1600

SDJ-021
White Magicial Hat
C $ .30

SDJ-022
Penguin Soldier
SR $ 3.00

SDJ-023
Thousand Dragon
C $ .30

SDJ-024
Flame Swordsman
C $ 1.50

MALEVOLENT NUZZLER

[MAGIC CARD]
A monster equipped with this card increases its ATK by 700 points. When this card is sent from the field to the Graveyard, you can pay 700 Life Points to place it on top of your Deck.

DARK HOLE

[MAGIC CARD]
Destroys all monsters on the field.

DIAN KETO THE CURE MASTER

[MAGIC CARD]
Increases your Life Points by 1000 points.

FISSURE

[MAGIC CARD]
Destroys 1 opponent's face-up monster with the lowest ATK.

SDJ-025
Malevolent Nuzzler
C $ .30

SDJ-026
Dark Hole
C $ .30

SDJ-027
Dian Keto the Cure
Master
C $ .30

SDJ-028
Fissure
C $ .30

DE-SPELL

[MAGIC CARD]
Destroys 1 Magic Card on the field. If this card's target is face-down, flip it face-up. If the card is a Magic Card, it is destroyed. If not, it is returned to its face-down position. The flipped card is not activated.

CHANGE OF HEART

[MAGIC CARD]
Select and control 1 opposing monster (regardless of position) on the field until the end of your turn.

BLOCK ATTACK

[MAGIC CARD]
Select 1 of your opponent's monsters and shift it to Defense Position.

GIANT TRUNADE

[MAGIC CARD]
Returns all Magic and Trap Cards on the field to the respective owner's hand.

SDJ-029
De-Spell
C $ .30

SDJ-030
Change of Heart
C $ .30

SDJ-031
Block Attack
C $ .30

SDJ-032
Giant Trunade
C $ .30

THE RELIABLE GUARDIAN [MAGIC CARD]

Increase 1 monster's DEF by 700 points during the turn this card is activated.

SDJ-033
The Reliable Guardian
C $ .30

REMOVE TRAP [MAGIC CARD]

Destroys 1 face-up Trap Card on the field.

SDJ-034
Remove Trap
C $ .30

MONSTER REBORN [MAGIC CARD]

Select 1 Monster Card from either your opponent's or your own Graveyard and place it on the field under your control in Attack or Defense Position (face-up). This is considered a Special Summon.

SDJ-035
Monster Reborn
C $ .80

POLYMERIZATION [MAGIC CARD]

Fuses 2 or more Fusion-Material Monsters to form a new Fusion Monster.

SDJ-036
Polymerization
C $ 4.00

MOUNTAIN [MAGIC CARD]

Increases the ATK and DEF of all Dragon, Winged Beast, and Thunder-Type monsters by 200 points.

SDJ-037
Mountain
C $ .30

DRAGON TREASURE [MAGIC CARD]

A Dragon-Type monster equipped with this card increases its ATK and DEF by 300 points.

SDJ-038
Dragon Treasure
C $ .30

ETERNAL REST [MAGIC CARD]

Destroys all monsters equipped with Equip Cards.

SDJ-039
Eternal Rest
C $ .30

SHIELD & SWORD [MAGIC CARD]

For 1 turn, each face-up monster's original ATK becomes their original DEF and vice-versa. Any additions or subtractions to ATK and/or DEF due to card effects are applied to the new ATK and DEF. Monsters summoned after this card's activation are excluded.

SDJ-040
Shield & Sword
C $ .30

SCAPEGOAT [MAGIC CARD]

When this card is activated, you cannot summon any monster in the same turn (including Flip Summon and Special Summon). Place 4 "Sheep Tokens" (Beast-Type/EARTH/Star 1/ATK 0/DEF 0) in Defense Position on your side of the field. The tokens cannot be used as a Tribute for a Tribute Summon.

SDJ-041
Scapegoat
SR $ 2.50

JUST DESSERTS [TRAP CARD]

Inflict 500 points of Direct Damage to your opponent's Life Points for each monster your opponent has on the field.

SDJ-042
Just Desserts
C $ .30

TRAP HOLE [TRAP CARD]

If the ATK of a monster summoned by your opponent (excluding Special Summon) is 1000 points or more, the monster is destroyed.

SDJ-043
Trap Hole
C $ .30

REINFORCEMENTS [TRAP CARD]

Increase 1 selected monster's ATK by 500 points during the turn this card is activated.

SDJ-044
Reinforcements
C $ .30

CASTLE WALLS 罠
[TRAP CARD]

Increase a selected monster's DEF by 500 points during the turn this card is activated.

SDJ-045
Castle Walls
C $ .30

WABOKU 罠
[TRAP CARD]

Any damage inflicted by an opponent's monster is decreased to 0 during the turn this card is activated.

SDJ-046
Waboku
C $ .30

ULTIMATE OFFERING 罠
[TRAP CARD]

At the cost of 500 Life Points per monster, a player is allowed an extra Normal Summon or Set.

SDJ-047
Ultimate Offering
C $ .30

SEVEN TOOLS OF THE BANDIT 罠
[TRAP CARD]

Pay 1000 of your Life Points to negate the activation of a Trap Card and destroy it.

SDJ-048
Seven Tools of the
Bandit
C $ .30

FAKE TRAP 罠
[TRAP CARD]

When your opponent uses a Magic, Trap, or Effect Monster Card to destroy your Trap Card(s), this card can be destroyed as a substitute for your Trap Card(s).

SDJ-049
Fake Trap
C $ .30

REVERSE TRAP 罠
[TRAP CARD]

All increases and decreases to ATK and DEF are reversed for the turn in which this card is activated.

SDJ-050
Reverse Trap
C $ .30

RYU-RAN 炎

[DRAGON]
A vicious little dragon sheltered in an egg that looks deceptively harmless.

ATK/2200 DEF/2600

SDP-003
Ryu-Ran
C $ .30

ILLUSIONIST FACELESS MAGE 闇

[SPELLCASTER]
Manipulates enemy attacks with the power of illusion.

ATK/1200 DEF/2200

SDP-004
Illusionist Faceless Mage
C $ .30

ROGUE DOLL 光

[SPELLCASTER]
A deadly doll gifted with mystical power, it is particularly powerful when attacking against dark forces.

ATK/1600 DEF/1000

SDP-005
Rogue Doll
C $ .30

URABY 地

[DINOSAUR]
Fast on its feet, this dinosaur rips enemies to shreds with its sharp claws.

ATK/1500 DEF/ 800

SDP-006
Uraby
C $ .30

GIANT SOLDIER OF STONE 地

[ROCK]
A giant warrior made of stone. A punch from this creature has earth-shaking results.

ATK/1300 DEF/2000

SDP-007
Giant Soldier of Stone
C $ .30

AQUA MADOOR 水

[SPELLCASTER]
A wizard of the waters that conjures a liquid wall to crush any enemies that oppose him.

ATK/1200 DEF/2000

SDP-008
Aqua Madoor
C $ .30

TOON ALLIGATOR 水

[REPTILE]
An alligator monster straight from the cartoons.

ATK/ 800 DEF/1600

SDP-009
Toon Alligator
C $ .60

HANE-HANE 地

[BEAST/EFFECT]
FLIP: Select 1 Monster Card on the field, irregardless of position and return it to its owner's hand.

ATK/ 450 DEF/ 500

SDP-010
Hane-Hane
C $ .30

SONIC BIRD 風

[WINGED BEAST/EFFECT]
When this card is summoned (excluding Special Summon), you may move 1 Ritual Magic Card from your Deck to your hand. The Deck is then shuffled.

ATK/1400 DEF/1000

SDP-011
Sonic Bird
C $ .30

JIGEN BAKUDAN 炎

[PYRO/EFFECT]
FLIP: After this card is flipped, offer it as a Tribute during your Standby Phase to destroy all monsters on your side of the field and inflict Direct Damage equal to half of the total ATK of the destroyed cards (excluding this monster) to your opponent's Life Points.

ATK/ 200 DEF/1000

SDP-012
Jigen Bakudan
C $ .30

MASK OF DARKNESS 闇

[FIEND/EFFECT]
FLIP: Select 1 Trap Card from your Graveyard and return it to your hand.

ATK/ 900 DEF/ 400

SDP-013
Mask of Darkness
C $ .30

WITCH OF THE BLACK FOREST 闇

[SPELLCASTER/EFFECT]
When this card is sent from the field to the Graveyard, move 1 monster with a DEF of 1500 or less from your Deck to your hand. Your Deck is then shuffled.

ATK/1100 DEF/1200

SDP-014
Witch of the Black Forest
C $ .40

Man-Eater Bug
[INSECT/EFFECT]
FLIP: Destroys 1 monster on the field regardless of position.

ATK/ 450 DEF/ 600

SDP-015
Man-Eater Bug
C $ .30

Muka Muka
[ROCK/EFFECT]
Increase the ATK and DEF of this card by 300 points for every card in your hand.

ATK/ 600 DEF/ 300

SDP-016
Muka Muka
C $ .30

Dream Clown
[WARRIOR/EFFECT]
When this card is changed from Attack Position to Defense Position, select and destroy 1 monster on your opponent's side of the field.

ATK/1200 DEF/ 900

SDP-017
Dream Clown
C $ .30

Armed Ninja
[WARRIOR/EFFECT]
FLIP: Destroys 1 Magic Card on the field. If this card's target is face-down, flip it face-up. If the card is a Magic Card, it is destroyed. If not, it is returned to its face-down position. The flipped card is not activated.

ATK/ 300 DEF/ 300

SDP-018
Armed Ninja
C $ .30

Hiro's Shadow Scout
[FIEND/EFFECT]
FLIP: Your opponent draws 3 cards. Both players check the cards and any Magic Cards among them must be immediately discarded to the Graveyard.

ATK/ 650 DEF/ 500

SDP-019
Hiro's Shadow Scout
C $ .30

Blue-Eyes Toon Dragon
[DRAGON/TOON]
This card cannot be summoned unless "Toon World" is on the field. This card cannot attack in the same turn that it is summoned. Pay 500 Life Points each time this monster attacks. When "Toon World" is destroyed, this card is also destroyed. If your opponent doesn't control a Toon monster on the field, this card may inflict Direct Damage to your opponent's Life Points. If a Toon monster is on your opponent's side of the field, your attacks must target the Toon monster.

ATK/3000 DEF/2500

SDP-020
Blue Eyes Toon
Dragon
C $ 7.00

Toon Summoned Skull
[FIEND/TOON]
This card cannot be summoned unless "Toon World" is on the field. This card cannot attack in the same turn that it is summoned. Pay 500 Life Points each time this monster attacks. When "Toon World" is destroyed, this card is also destroyed. If your opponent doesn't control a Toon monster on the field, this card may inflict Direct Damage to your opponent's Life Points. If a Toon monster is on your opponent's side of the field, your attacks must target the Toon monster.

ATK/2500 DEF/1200

SDP-021
Toon Summoned Skull
C $ .30

Manga Ryu-Ran
[DRAGON/TOON]
This card cannot be summoned unless "Toon World" is on the field. This card cannot attack in the same turn that it is summoned. Pay 500 Life Points each time this monster attacks. When "Toon World" is destroyed, this card is also destroyed. If your opponent doesn't control a Toon monster on the field, this card may inflict Direct Damage to your opponent's Life Points. If a Toon monster is on your opponent's side of the field, your attacks must target the Toon monster.

ATK/2200 DEF/2600

SDP-022
Manga Ryu-Ran
C $ .30

Toon Mermaid
[AQUA/TOON]
This card cannot be summoned unless "Toon World" is on the field. This card cannot attack in the same turn that it is summoned. When "Toon World" is destroyed, this card is also destroyed. If your opponent doesn't control a Toon monster on the field, this card may inflict Direct Damage to your opponent's Life Points. If a Toon monster is on your opponent's side of the field, your attacks must target the Toon monster.

ATK/1400 DEF/1500

SDP-023
Toon Mermaid
C $ .40

Toon World
[MAGIC CARD]
This card is activated by paying 1000 of your Life Points.

SDP-024
Toon World
C $ .30

Black Pendant
[MAGIC CARD]
A monster equipped with this card increases its ATK by 500 points. When this card is sent from the field to the Graveyard, inflict 500 points of Direct Damage to your opponent's Life Points.

SDP-025
Black Pendant
C $ .30

Dark Hole
[MAGIC CARD]
Destroys all monsters on the field.

SDP-026
Dark Hole
C $ .80

DIAN KETO THE CURE MASTER

[MAGIC CARD]

Increases your Life Points by 1000 points.

FISSURE

[MAGIC CARD]

Destroys 1 opponent's face-up monster with the lowest ATK.

DE-SPELL

[MAGIC CARD]

Destroys 1 Magic Card on the field. If this card's target is face-down, flip it face-up. If the card is a Magic Card, it is destroyed. If not, it is returned to its face-down position. The flipped card is not activated.

CHANGE OF HEART

[MAGIC CARD]

Select and control 1 opposing monster (regardless of position) on the field until the end of your turn.

SDP-027
Dian Keto the Cure
Master
C $ .30

SDP-028
Fissure
C $ .30

SDP-029
De-Spell
C $ .30

SDP-030
Change of Heart
C $ .30

STOP DEFENSE

[MAGIC CARD]

Select 1 of your opponent's monsters and switch it to Attack Position. If the card is face-down, flip it face-up. If the card has a flip effect, it is activated immediately.

MYSTICAL SPACE TYPHOON

[MAGIC CARD]

Destroy 1 Magic or Trap Card on the field.

RUSH RECKLESSLY

[MAGIC CARD]

Increase 1 monster's ATK by 700 points during the turn this card is activated.

REMOVE TRAP

[MAGIC CARD]

Destroys 1 face-up Trap Card on the field.

SDP-031
Stop Defense
C $ .30

SDP-032
Mystical Space
Typhoon
C $ .30

SDP-033
Rush Recklessly
C $ .30

SDP-034
Remove Trap
C $ .30

MONSTER REBORN

[MAGIC CARD]

Select 1 Monster Card from either your opponent's or your own Graveyard and place it on the field under your control in Attack or Defense Position (face-up). This is considered a Special Summon.

SOUL RELEASE

[MAGIC CARD]

Select up to 5 cards from either you or your opponent's Graveyard and remove them from the current Duel.

YAMI

[MAGIC CARD]

Increases the ATK and DEF of all Fiend and Spellcaster-Type monsters by 200 points. Also decreases the ATK and DEF of all Fairy-Type monsters by 200 points.

BLACK ILLUSION RITUAL

[MAGIC CARD]

This card is used to Ritual Summon "Relinquished". You must also offer monsters whose total Level Stars equal 1 or more from the field or your hand as a Tribute.

SDP-035
Monster Reborn
C $ 1.00

SDP-036
Soul Release
C $ .30

SDP-037
Yami
C $ .30

SDP-038
Black Illusion Ritual
C $ .30

SDP-039
Ring of Magnetism
C $ .30

SDP-040
Graceful Charity
SR $ 3.50

SDP-041
Trap Hole
C $ .30

SDP-042
Reinforcements
C $ .30

SDP-043
Castle Walls
C $ .30

SDP-044
Waboku
C $ .30

SDP-045
Seven Tools of the
Bandit
C $ .30

SDP-046
Ultimate Offering
C $ .30

SDP-047
Robbin' Goblin
C $ .30

SDP-048
Magic Jammer
C $ 4.50

SDP-049
Enchanted Javelin
C $ .30

SDP-050
Gryphon Wing
SR $ 1.30

WHAT IS A STAPLE CARD?

By Professor Duel

Just what is a Staple Card?

Is it a card with a staple in it? Or maybe it's a staple with a card in it? No silly, it's a card that has value and can improve any deck. Although there are many cards out now—and lots of cool cards still to come—that can be considered a staple card in certain types of decks, we will only be talking about staple cards referred to as my Big 6 staple cards, and a few other cards that are good in any kind of deck.

My Big 6 staple cards are Raigeki, Dark Hole, Mirror Force, Monster Reborn, Change of Heart, and Pot of Greed. All of these cards are limited to one per deck and all of the cards deserve a place in your deck.

Raigeki

Raigeki is a super rare magic card found in the Legend of Blue Eyes booster series, card number LOB-053. This card destroys all the monsters on your opponent's side of the field. There really isn't much to say about this card other than IT ROCKS! What more could you want?

Dark Hole

Dark Hole is a super rare magic card found in the Legend of Blue Eyes booster series and also a common card found in all the starter decks. For the Legend of Blue Eyes booster series the card number is LOB-052.

Dark Hole is almost like Raigeki, but instead of destroying only your opponent's monsters, it destroys all the monsters on the field – including YOURS. Dark Hole is a great card to use when:

• You have no monsters on the field.
• You are launching all your monsters for Cannon Soldier.
• You are going second.
• Your opponent is almost out of life points and you just need to get in that last attack.

Change of Heart

Change of Heart is an ultra rare magic card from the Metal Raiders booster series and also a common card found in all of the starter decks. For the Metal Raider booster series the card number is MRD-060.

Change of Heart lets you assume control over one of your opponent's monsters for one turn. While you have the card under your control you may use the card as if it was your own. If the card has a flip effect, you may use it and get the effect yourself. If you want to bring out one of your tribute monsters, you may use your opponent's monster as a tribute to bring out one of your own. If you have a Cannon Solider or Amazon Archer out on the field, you may use the effect of these cards on your opponent's monster as well. Change of Heart is also a great card to get the one monster out of the way and attack your opponent's life points directly— with his own monster (it's the ultimate insult)!

Mirror Force

Mirror Force is an ultra rare trap card found in the Metal Raiders booster series, card number MRD-138. Mirror Force takes the attack of one of your opponent's monsters and sends it back to him, and destroys all his monsters in attack position. This is a really awesome card! I mean you have no monsters out, you're about to lose the game, but wait you have Mirror

Force down and you've just used it to destroy all your opponent's monsters. BAM! Now you're back in this duel, all because of one great card.

Monster Reborn

Monster Reborn is an ultra rare magic card found in the Legend of Blue Eyes booster series and also a common card found in all the starter decks. In the Legend of Blue Eyes booster series the card number is LOB-118.

This card lets you bring back one monster from either you or your opponent's graveyard. There are not enough words to describe how useful this card is, but I'll try. Let's say your opponent had a Blue Eyes out on the field and you destroyed it with a Raigeki. Yeah! NOW you can bring it back under your own control and use it against him, mmmuhahaha! Do you need to know anything else?

Pot of Greed

Pot of Greed is a rare magic card found in the Legend of Blue Eyes booster series, card number LOB-119. There's just one thing you should know: Greed is good!

This card lets you draw two extra cards the turn you use it. In the game of Yu-Gi-Oh, speed is a very crucial component. The quicker you can get to the cards that you need, the faster you can win the duel. That is why cards like this are so crucial to have in your deck. More cards equals more options, enough said.

The Rest

Besides the Big 6 there are also other cards that can greatly improve any deck. These cards include Cyber-Jar, Imperial Order, Premature Burial, Graceful Charity, Call of the Haunted, Sangan, Witch of the Black Forest, Sinister Serpent, Axe of Despair, Snatch Steal, Jinzo, Magic Cylinder, Harpies Feather Duster, Swords of Revealing Light, Creature Swap, Exiled Force, Heavy Storm, Torrential Tribute, and Fiber-Jar. With the exception of Graceful Charity, which is limited to 2 per deck, and Axe of Despair, which isn't limited at all. All the cards listed are restricted to one per deck.

Just remember a staple card is just a card that is indispensable to your deck or a card that can turn the duel around on its own. As you become more experienced, you'll learn which cards help you most, and you'll always make sure they're in your deck. Without staple cards a deck will just fall apart in a duel. That's why they call them STAPLES!

ULTIMATE CARD COMBOS

HEAVY METAL CARD COMBOS THAT ARE AS AFFORDABLE AS THEY ARE EFFECTIVE

Getting started in Yu-Gi-Oh can be difficult. How can you get into the game without paying a huge amount of money? The answer is simple, just read on. These Ultimate Combos offers many possibilities within the game, for the beginning player to the master duelist. Enter "Metal Raider," an affordable booster pack with enough combinations to build your deck. Let's take a look at them now…

CARD COMBO: FREE REBORN.

Key Cards:
MRD-036 Magician of Faith and SDK-036 Monster Reborn

Combo Procedure:
Set MRD-036 Magician of Faith in face-down defense position first. On the next turn, play SDK-036 Monster Reborn. Select a Monster Card from one of the player's Graveyard. Special Summon a monster onto the Field from the Graveyard and take control of it. Flip MRD-036 Magician of Faith in face-up position, search your Graveyard for a SDK-036 Monster Reborn and add it to your hand.

STRENGTH:

SDK-036 Monster Reborn is limited to 1 per deck ONLY. By using this combo, you may use SDK-036 Monster Reborn for 2 times and Special Summon 2 Monsters from the Graveyard to the Field in the same turn.

WEAKNESS:

If MRD-036 Magician of Faith is destroyed by LOB-052 Dark Hole, LOB-053 Raigeki or LON-025 Torrential Tribute in face-down position, the flip effect won't be activated.

CARD COMBO: GREEDY EYE.

Key Cards:
MRD-017 Big Eye and TP3-014 Pot of Greed

Combo Procedure:
Set MRD-017 Big Eye in face-down defense position first. On the next turn, flip MRD-017 Big Eye in face-up position. Look at the next 5 cards of your deck. Rearrange them in any order you like and replace them on the top of your deck. Play TP3-014 Pot of Greed and draw 2 cards from the top of your deck.

STRENGTH:

You can manage what you are going to draw on the next few turns.

WEAKNESS:

If MRD-017 Big Eye is destroyed by LOB-052 Dark Hole, LOB-053 Raigeki or LON-025 Torrential Tribute in face-down position, the flip effect won't be activated.

CARD COMBO: THREE THOUSAND RECOVERIES.

Key Cards:
MRD-099 Immortal of Thunder and SDK-046 Hane-Hane

Combo Procedure:
Set MRD-099 Immortal of Thunder and SDK-046 Hane-Hane in face-down defense position first. On the next turn, flip MRD-099 Immortal of Thunder in face-up position, increase your Life Points by 3,000 points and flip SDK-046 Hane-Hane in face-up position. Target MRD-099 Immortal of Thunder on the field and return it to your hand.

STRENGTH:
Make sure you have LOB-101 Swords of Revealing Light on the field whenever you want to activate this combo. You can activate LOB-101 Swords of Revealing Light to protect your MRD-099 Immortal of Thunder on the Field.

WEAKNESS:
If MRD-099 Immortal of Thunder is sent from the field to Graveyard, you will decrease your Life Points by 5,000 points.

CARD COMBO: CHEAP SUMMONS.

Key Cards:
MRD-057 Tribute to the Doomed, SDK-036 Monster Reborn and PSV-000 Jinzo

Combo Procedure:
Play MRD-057 Tribute to the Doomed, discard PSV-000 Jinzo from your Hand to the Graveyard and destroy a Monster on the Field (Regardless of Position). Then, activate SDK-036 Monster Reborn and target PSV-000 Jinzo from your Graveyard and Special Summon it on the Field.

STRENGTH:
Quick Summon on Level 5+ monster from your Hand to the Field.

WEAKNESS:
MRD-057 Tribute to the Doomed can be negated by MRD-128 Magic Jammer or PSV-104 Imperial Order.

CARD COMBO: OUT GAME.

Key Cards:
SDY-042 Card Destruction and LOB-065 Gravedigger Ghoul

Combo Procedure:
Activate SDY-042 Card Destruction, both players must discard their entire hands and draw the same number of cards that they discarded from their respective Decks. Then, activate LOB-065 Gravedigger Ghoul and select 2 Monster Cards from your opponent's Graveyard.

STRENGTH:
These Monster Cards are removed from play for the remainder of the Duel. Remove key monster of your opponent's, so he/she cannot reborn it.

WEAKNESS:
SDY-042 Card Destruction and LOB-065 Gravedigger Ghoul can be negated by MRD-128 Magic Jammer or PSV-104 Imperial Order.

CARD COMBO: DOUBLE THEFT.

Key Cards:
MRD-135 Robbin' Goblin and MRD-016 White Magical Hat

Combo Procedure:
Summon MRD-016 White Magical Hat and activate MRD-135 Robbin' Goblin. Whenever
MRD-016 White Magical Hat inflicts damage to your opponent's Life Points, your opponent must randomly discard 1 card from his
Hand and you get to discard 1 more card from his Hand by the effect of MRD-135 Robbin' Goblin.

STRENGTH:
You are able to discard 2 cards from your opponent's Hand by a single attack. Another selection of Hand Destruction Deck!

WEAKNESS:
MRD-016 White Magical Hat has 1000 points of ATK only. It is hard to inflict damage to your opponent's Life Points unless he/she has an empty field.

CARD COMBO: SIDE MIRROR.

Key Cards:
MRD-138 Mirror Force and MRD-014 Mask of Darkness

Combo Procedure:
Set MRD-014 Mask of Darkness in face-down defense position first. On the next turn, activate MRD-138 Mirror Force when your opponent's Monster attacks. Destroy all of your opponent's Monsters in attack position. Next turn, flip MRD-014 Mask of Darkness in face-up on face-up position, search your Graveyard for MRD-138 Mirror Force and put it into your Hand.

STRENGTH:
Like Free Reborn, the only difference is MRD-014 Mask of Darkness returns a Trap Card from Graveyard to your Hand.

WEAKNESS:
If MRD-014 Mask of Darkness is destroyed by LOB-052 Dark Hole, LOB-053 Raigeki or LON-025 Torrential Tribute in face-down position, the flip effect won't be activated.

If you look at all cards in Metal Raider, you will find out the potential of chain combos. We have

MRD-014 Mask of Darkness, MRD-036 Magician of Faith and other flip effect monsters, all lined up

in face-down position. Your opponent has no way to know what combos you are hiding underneath.

Your opponent will be scared to attack because he/she fears it may be a Man-Eater Bug or Cyber

Jar. If you play our combos in your deck, your opponent will never know what will happen next.

ULTIMATE COMBOS

UNLOCKING THE TRUE POWER OF EXODIA

In every Yu-Gi-Oh set there are cards that make you think twice (sometimes more) about how to use them, and Exodia is no exception. You may wonder, "How do these cards work together effectively?" and we have the answer. In this section we will go over an abundance of Yu-Gi-Oh combos with you, from the traditional to the unheard of, discussing the strength and weakness of each one. Let's start with the Exodia deck.

CARD COMBO: ULTIMATE WINNING.

Key Cards: LOB-120 Right Leg of the Forbidden One, LOB-121 Left Leg of the Forbidden One, LOB-122 Right Arm of the Forbidden One, LOB-123 Left Arm of the Forbidden One and LOB-124 Exodia The Forbidden One.

Combo Procedure:
Grab these 5 cards in Hand by drawing naturally or search for them by MRD-069 Sangan or MRD-116 Witch of Black Forest's effect.

STRENGTH:

An automatic victory can be declared by the player whose Hand contains these cards together.

WEAKNESS:

If any pieces of Exodia are removed from play, you can be declared the loser in a few turns.

CARD COMBO: FLASH ATTACK.

Key Cards: LOB-053 Raigeki and LOB-001 Blue-Eyed White Dragon

Combo Procedure:
Summon LOB-001 Blue-Eyed White Dragon on the field and play LOB-053 Raigeki. LOB-053 Raigeki destroys all monsters on your opponent's side of the field. Attack your opponent's Life Points by LOB-001 Blue-Eyed White Dragon.

STRENGTH:

3,000 points of Direct Damage from LOB-001 Blue-Eyed White Dragon.

WEAKNESS:

TP3-002 Anti-Raigeki: When your opponent activates Raigeki, all of your opponent's monsters are destroyed in place of yours.

CARD COMBO: THE BURNING VILLAGE.

Key Cards:

3 x SDK-023 Ookazi

Combo Procedure:

Activate 3 pieces of SDK-023 Ookazi at the same time.

STRENGTH:

Inflict 2,400 points of Direct Damage to your opponent's Life Points.

WEAKNESS:

The cards in your Hand will be going very fast. Your opponent may negate this combo by PSV-104 Imperial Order.

CARD COMBO: RISE OF THE SKULL.

Key Cards:

SDY-032 Change of Heart and SDY-004 Summoned Skull

Combo Procedure:

Activate SDY-032 Change of Heart and take control of one of your opponent's monsters. Offer this monster as a tribute and Tribute Summon SDY-004 Summoned Skull.

STRENGTH:

Destroy one of your opponent's Monsters and Tribute Summon a Level 6 monster at the same time.

WEAKNESS:

If your opponent does not have any monster on the field, you cannot use this combo.

CARD COMBO: INJECTION MASTER DIAN KETO.

Key Cards:

3 x SDY-023 Dian Keto The Cure Master

Combo Procedure:

Activate 3 pieces of SDY-023 Dian Keto The Cure Master at the same time.

STRENGTH:

Increases 3,000 Life Points within a turn.

WEAKNESS:

The cards in your Hand will be going very fast. Your opponent may negate this combo by PSV-104 Imperial Order.

CARD COMBO: CHAOS ATTACK

Key Cards:
LOB-052 Dark Hole and LOB-007 Celtic Guardian

Combo Procedure:
Play LOB-052 Dark Hole and destroy all monsters on the field. Summon LOB-007 Celtic Guardian and attack your opponent's Life Points.

STRENGTH:

1,400 points of Direct Damage from LOB-007 Celtic Guardian.

WEAKNESS:

TP1-005 White Hole: When your opponent plays LOB-052 Dark Hole, the monsters on your side of the field are not destroyed.

CARD COMBO: DARK POWER REVIVAL.

Key Cards: SDY-042 Card Destruction, LOB-118 Monster Reborn and LOB-005 Dark Magician

Combo Procedure:
Activate SDY-042 Card Destruction to discard LOB-005 Dark Magician from your hand to the Graveyard. Play LOB-118 Monster Reborn and Special Summoned LOB-005 Dark Magician from your Graveyard to the Field.

STRENGTH:

Beside Tribute Summon, you can Special Summon LOB-005 Dark Magician easily.

WEAKNESS:

You will discard other good cards when you activate SDY-042 Card Destruction to discard LOB-005 Dark Magician from your hand to the Graveyard.

Whatever combinations you use, enjoy your flavors of combo. The times may have changed, but the good combo remains.

The Master DUELIST!

ASPECT OF PLAY

Understanding how to use Chain Reactions in the Yu-Gi-Oh! TCG

No doubt one of the most-confusing aspects of the Yu-Gi-Oh! TCG is the "Chain Rule." For beginners to the game (or those who have not played Magic: The Gathering), it can be difficult to understand. Put simply, the Chain Rule is the sequence by which you play your cards in response to an opponent's actions. Whenever your opponent takes virtually any action, you have the option to "Chain," that is, respond to your opponent's move. You are not limited to only negating the card that your opponent played in order to Chain, nor are you required to target the specific card your opponent played (unless, of course, the card you play is a counter-trap, in which event it must target the trap card that your opponent last played).

The key to the whole thing is "Spell Speed." The official rules of Yu-Gi-Oh! provide for three different levels of "Spell Speed." Normal Magic, Equipment Magic, Field Magic, All Played Effects and Monster Effects at the time of a Flip Summon are all Spell Speed level 1. Quickplay Magic, Normal Traps and Monster Effects at the time of being Triggered are all Spell Speed level 2. Counter-Traps are all Spell Speed level 3. When your

opponent plays any of those cards, you have the option to "Chain" with one of your own effects. There are two basic rules to remember: (1) Spell Speed level 1 card can not chain (so you can't, for example, play a Dark Hole when your opponent uses a Raigeki); and (2) you can only chain with items that have an equal or higher spell speed level than that the card your opponent played. And remember, summoning and/or attacking are also valid chaining actions.

So what does this all mean? Probably the best way to explain is by way of example. Suppose your opponent activates a Normal Trap (which automatically has a Spell Speed level of 2). You can now chain with one of your own cards that has an equal or greater Spell Speed. You can now use cards or effects that have a Spell Speed of 2 or 3. So, for example, you could now use your own Normal Trap card. The chain will continue in this fashion so long as a player keeps wishing to place a card in the chain. When all players are finished, the effects are then executed in the reverse order in which the cards were played, that is, you start with the effects of the last card played, then proceed backwards until you get to the first card in the chain. Any negated cards simply don't have an effect—they are skipped, while you proceed to the next card in the Chain. Here's an example:

PLAYER 1: PLAYS RAIGEKI
PLAYER 2: PLAYS MAGIC JAMMER
PLAYER 1: PLAYS 7 TOOLS
PLAYER 2: TAKES NO ACTION

The chain then "resolves" in reverse order as follows: First, 7 Tools (the last card in the chain) negates the Magic Jammer so that it is removed from the chain. The chain proceeds to the next card, Raigeki, which destroys all of Player 2's monster cards on the Field. Don't forget that it is 100% legal for you to Chain with a card that is about to be destroyed. For example, if your opponent plays Mystical Space Typhoon to destroy your face-down Waboku, it is still legal for you to

activate the Waboku and gain its effect before the Typhoon destroys it. Also remember that when the target of a card is removed before the card is resolved, or if the target of the card becomes illegal, the card's effect ends, and it is discarded. You can not choose another target for the card.

Three other things to remember: (1) once a chain ends, neither player can add any additional cards to that chain, (2) you can chain your own cards when your opponent has not done so (for example, if you play Card Destruction and your opponent does not chain, you can play Tailor of the Fickle from your hand), and (3) all card plays within the chain must still be legal (for example, if you play a Mystical Space Typhoon to destroy a face-down Mirror Force during your Main Phase 1, your opponent can not chain with the Mirror Force because Mirror Force can only be activated when an attack happens).

Although the concept of chaining is a difficult one, it is worth investing the time to thoroughly understand this VERY IMPORTANT aspect of the TCG. Once you have mastered it, you are well on your way to becoming a master duelist.

What are God Cards?

The ultimate guide to the greatest God Cards in the Yu-Gi-Oh! TCG. Find out what they are, where they come from and how you can use them in a duel.

What are the God Cards of Yu-Gi-Oh?

In the Cartoon and Comics, Maxamillion Pegasus found out about the God Cards in the history of Egypt. The ancient Egyptians sealed the God Cards in the stone tablets. Pegasus released that power and transforms the stone to three God Cards. However, Pegasus realized the power of God Cards has the power to destroy the world, so he hides the God Cards in the Tomb of Yami Yugi.

Where do the God Cards come from?

On April 17th, 2003, the Yu-Gi-Oh Worldwide Edition: *Stairways to the Destiny*, on the Gameboy Advanced was released in Japan. With support for English, French, Spanish, German, Japanese and Italian, duelists are no longer bound by the limitations of language. In the all-new adventure mode, enter the Battle City Tournament and challenge duelists around town to win the championship! However, Konami announced that God Cards are banned in any Tournament, due to the fact that the back of the God Card is different than other Yu-Gi-Oh cards. God Cards do not have any logo or letter of Yu-Gi-Oh written on the back. Also, the Card Effect of God cards are not written on the card, there are only monster descriptions on it.

How to use God Cards in a Duel!

Generally, you are not allowed to use God Cards in the Upper Deck Tournament. But you can use them when playing with your friends.

There are 3 rules to using them in a Duel.

A. Offer 3 monster cards on your Field to Summon a God card.

B. Monster, Magic and Trap effects that are designated targets on God Cards can last for one turn only.

C. Unless those Card Effects destroy God Cards on the Field, Card Effects can affect God Cards for one turn only. Example: your opponent uses Dark Hole, Mirror Force and Torrential Tribute on your God Card. The God Card is destroyed and it won't be coming back at the end of the turn.

How much does a God Card cost?

The God Cards are not for sale at your local card shop, but you may find them online. They cost $120-$150 USD each or $300-$400 for a set. If you want to get God Cards for FREE, you can go to Millennium Duelist Kingdom. They give out FREE God Cards and booster packs every week in contests. The web address is www.millenniumduelistkingdom.com

Millenniums ago, the ancient Egyptians created God Cards to rule the world.

Now, Yugi has Silfer the Sky Dragon, Kaiba has Obelisk the Tormentor and Marik has The Winged Dragon of Ra. So who is the greatest God? Who knows?

Index Number: WWE-001
Card Name: Silfer the Sky Dragon
Level: 10
Attribute: God
Type: Divine Beast
ATK: X000
DEF: X000
Note: Effect Monster
Rarity: Secret Rare
Game Code: N/A

Description/Effect:
Calculate the ATK and DEF of this card by 1000 points for every card in your Hand.

Ghostmaster's Note:
The Card effect of Silfer works like MRD-107 Muka Muka, but it counts 1000 points ATK and DEF for every card in your Hand. If you like Muka Muka, you will love Silfer too.

Index Number: WWE-002
Card Name: Obelisk the Tormentor
Level: 10
Attribute: God
Type: Divine Beast
ATK: 4000
DEF: 4000
Note: Effect Monster
Rarity: Secret Rare
Game Code: N/A

Description/Effect:
Offer 2 Monster as a Tribute and destroy all monsters on your opponent's Field. This monster cannot attack on the turn it activate this effect.

Ghostmaster's Note:
A built-in Rageki effect! This Monster Card cannot attack on that turn, while this effect is activated on the same turn.

Index Number: WWE-003
Card Name: The Winged Dragon of Ra
Level: 10
Attribute: God
Type: Divine Beast
ATK: ????
DEF: ????
Note: Effect Monster
Rarity: Secret Rare
Game Code: N/A

Description/Effect:
This Monster Card's ATK and DEF are equal to the total amount of respective Monster Cards' original ATK, which is tributed to Tribute Summon The Winged Dragon of Ra. While this monster is on the field, pay 1000 Life Points and destroy one of your opponent's Monsters on the Field. Or, pay any amount of Life Points for Activation Cost and increase The Winged Dragon of Ra's ATK and DEF rating by the number of Life Points you paid on the same turn.

Ghostmaster's Note:
If you tribute three Summon Skull to Tribute Summon The Winged Dragon of Ra, it will have 7500 ATK and 3600 DEF (2500+2500+2500= 7500 and 1200+1200+1200=3600). However, if you Special Summon The Winged Dragon of Ra, it will have 0 ATK and 0 DEF. This is the worst part of the card. Also, you cannot use MRD-069 Sangan's Card Effect to search Sun Dragon - Ra from your Deck to your Hand, since ???? is an unknown number. If you pay 2000 Life Points to Ra, Ra will increase 2000 ATK on that turn.